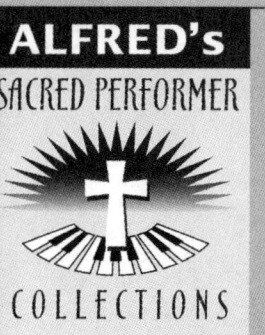

Wondrous Hymns, Book 1

8 Contemporary Arrangements of Traditional Hymns of Hope

Arranged by James Koerts

The day in which we live is filled with uncertainty and difficulties. All you have to do is pay attention to the continuous stream of news and it won't take long to realize that these are hard times. Natural disasters, the wickedness of man, and even good intentions have given way to destruction and devastation. Yet, in the midst of all this, a gentle ray of hope is freely offered to everyone. It is Jesus Christ, and if it weren't for His selfless sacrifice on the cross and His completed work at Calvary, we would certainly be hopeless.

Designed to reflect on the hope we have through Jesus, these arrangements remind us of the truth that we can trust in Him. He is a faithful and dependable God. Even when it appears that He is far from us, we have the promises of His word that remind us He will hear our prayers and be our strength.

James Koerts

Amazing Grace	2
Day by Day	12
He Leadeth Me	7
Jesus Is All the World to Me	22
Love Lifted Me	34
My Redeemer	16
Only Trust Him	40
'Tis So Sweet to Trust in Jesus	29

Alfred Music Publishing Co., Inc.
P.O. Box 10003
Van Nuys, CA 91410-0003
alfred.com

Copyright © MMXI by Alfred Music Publishing Co., Inc.
All rights reserved. Printed in USA.

No part of this book shall be reproduced, arranged, adapted, recorded, publicly performed, stored in a retrieval system, or transmitted by any means without written permission from the publisher. In order to comply with copyright laws, please apply for such written permission and/or license by contacting the publisher at alfred.com/permissions.

ISBN-10: 0-7390-6961-6
ISBN-13: 978-0-7390-6961-5

Amazing Grace

(Approx. Performance Time – 2:45)

from *Virginia Harmony,* 1831
Arr. James Koerts

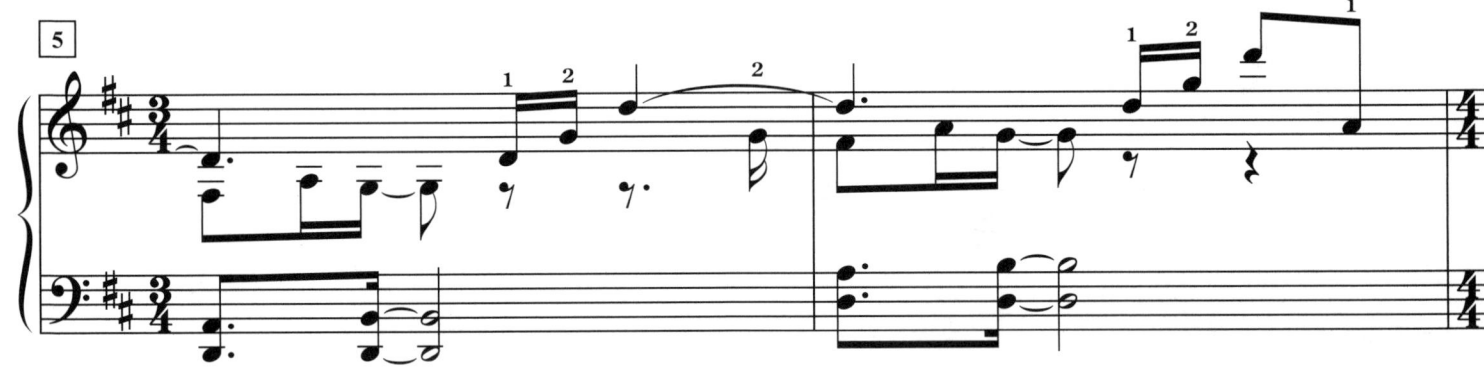

(Approx. Performance Time – 2:45)

HE LEADETH ME

William Bradbury
Arr. James Koerts

(Approx. Performance Time – 2:45)

dedicated to Beth, with love

Day by Day

Oscar Ahnfelt
Arr. James Koerts

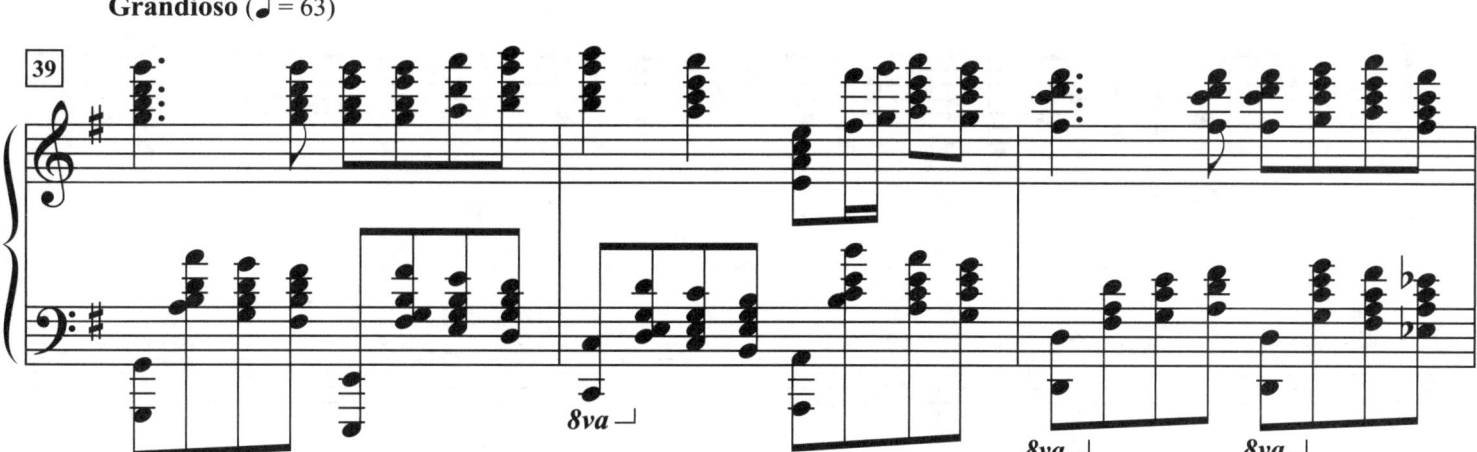

My Redeemer

(Approx. Performance Time – 2:30)

James McGranahan
Arr. James Koerts

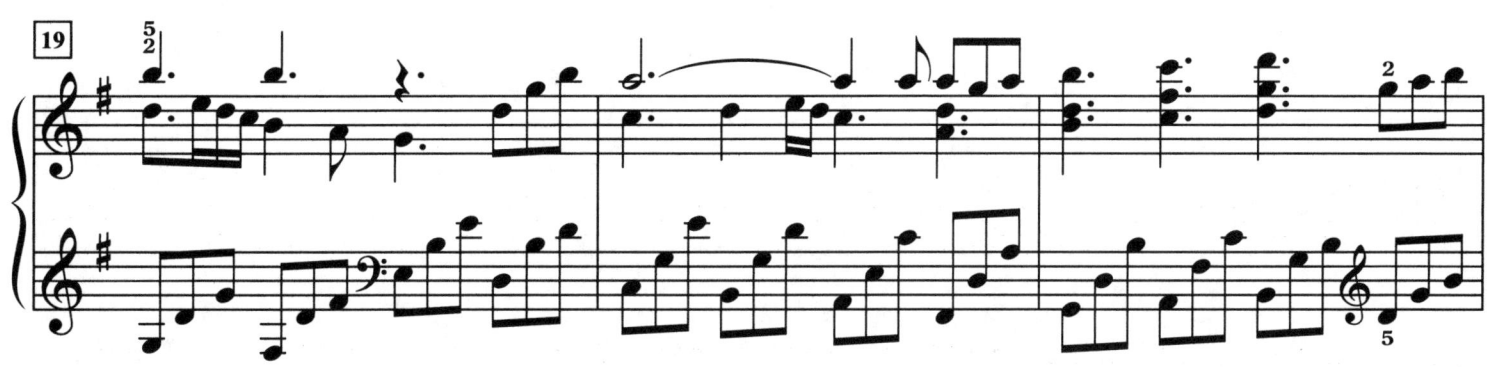

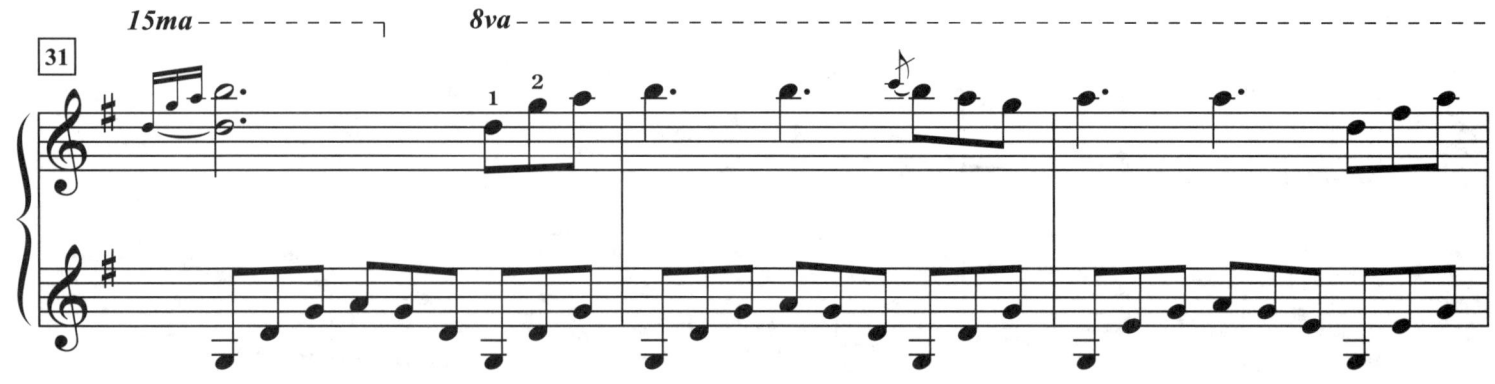

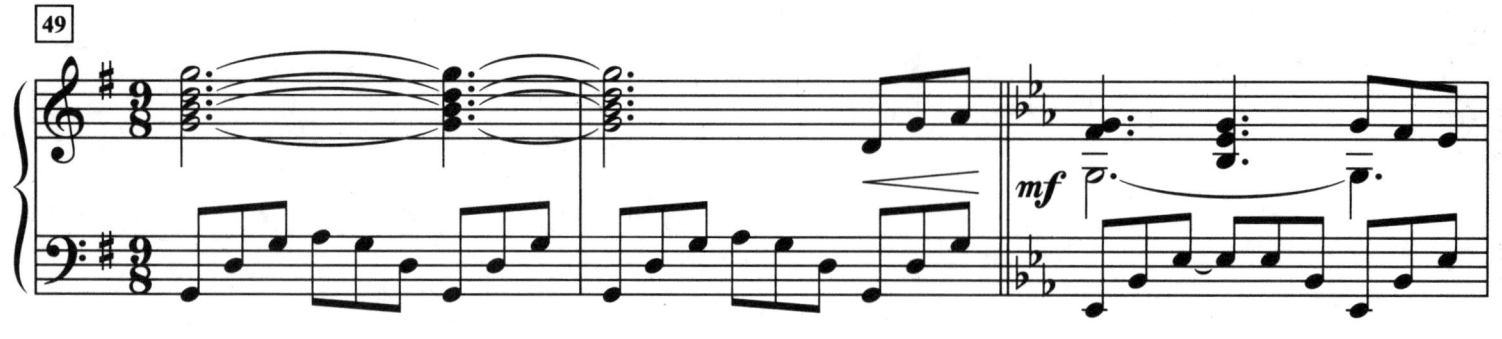

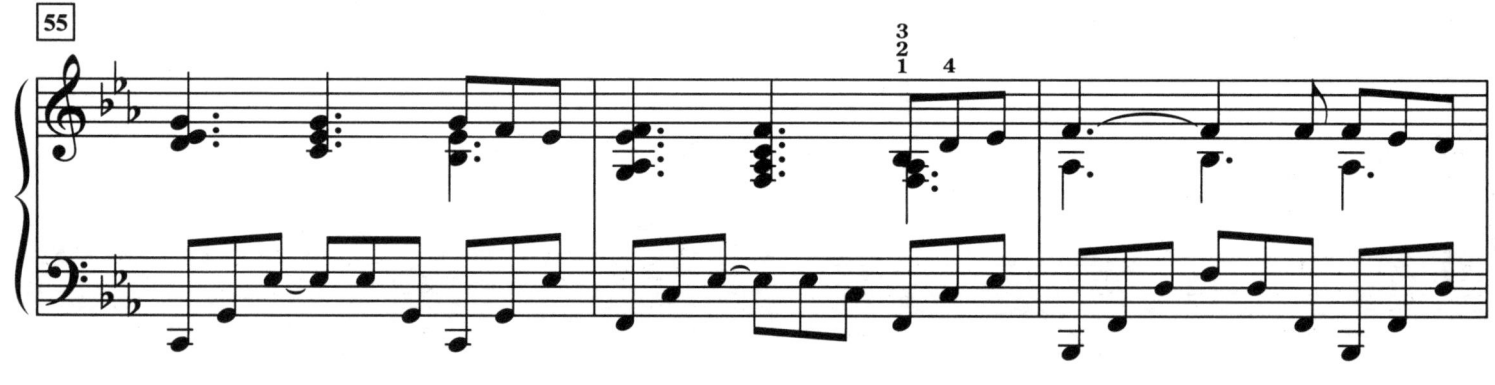
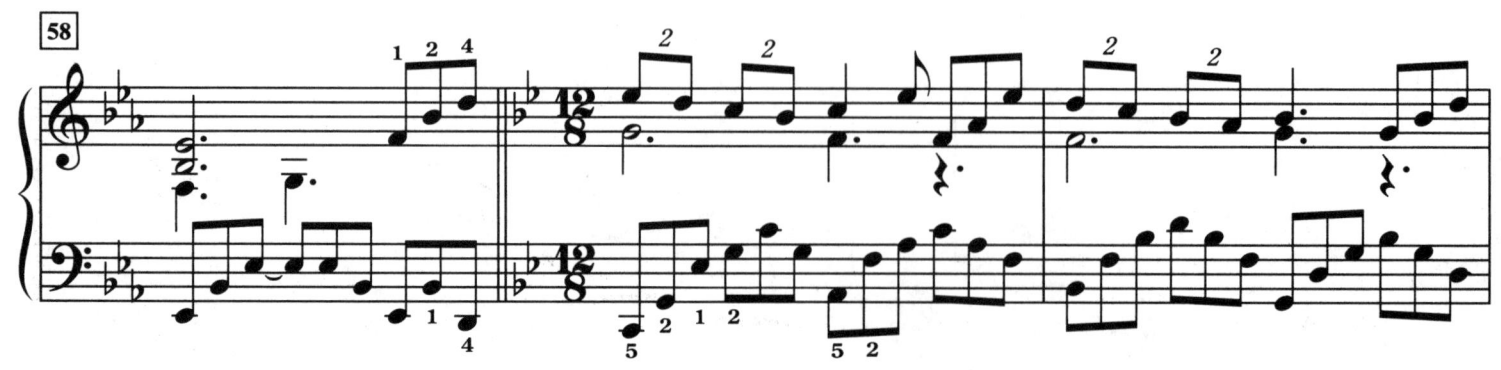

Jesus Is All the World to Me

(Approx. Performance Time – 3:00)

Will L. Thompson
Arr. James Koerts

for my daughter, Katelyn

'Tis So Sweet to Trust in Jesus

(Approx. Performance Time – 2:45)

William J. Kirkpatrick
Arr. James Koerts

(Approx. Performance Time – 4:15)

LOVE LIFTED ME

Howard Smith
Arr. James Koerts

Only Trust Him

(Approx. Performance Time – 2:30)

John Stockton
Arr. James Koerts

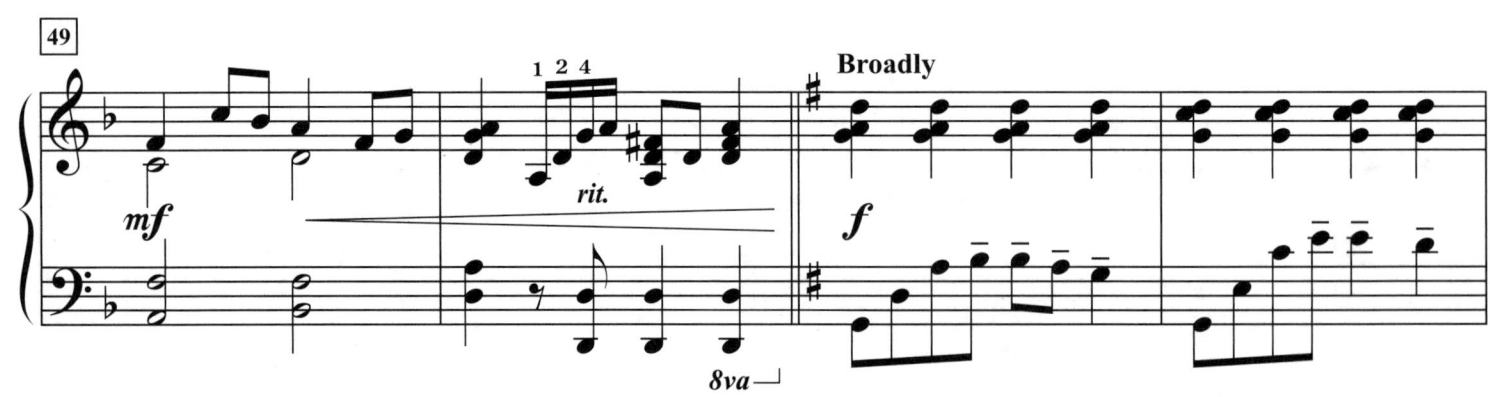